new holland horoscope series

LEO

2004

yasmin boland

NEW
HOLLAND

First published in Australia in 2003 by
New Holland Publishers (Australia) Pty Ltd
Sydney • Auckland • London • Cape Town

14 Aquatic Drive Frenchs Forest NSW 2086 Australia
218 Lake Road Northcote Auckland New Zealand
86 Edgware Road London W2 2EA United Kingdom
80 McKenzie Street Cape Town 8001 South Africa

10 9 8 7 6 5 4 3 2 1

The National Library of Australia Cataloguing-in-Publication Data

      Boland, Yasmin.
      Leo 2004.

      ISBN 1 74110 025 9.

      1. Leo (Astrology). 2. Horoscopes. I. Title.
      (Series: New Holland horoscope series).

      133.5266

Publishing Manager: Anouska Good
Senior Editor: Monica Ban
Designer: Karlman Roper
Astrology consultant: Martin Lipson
Printer: McPhersons Printing Group, Victoria

CONTENTS

HOW TO USE THIS BOOK

This book features a personality profile for your star sign, as well as forecasts for 2004 regarding love, career, money, and your life lessons. Also included are detailed week by week forecasts, giving you a flavour of the ever-changing heavens, as well as my Moon Meditations—ideas to think about, depending on the astroclimate at the time of the New and Full Moons. I'm a big believer in the power of the New Moon—and I hope you will be too, by the end of the year.

There's one New Moon per month (except 'once in a "Blue Moon"' when there are two!) and they give us the celestial opportunity to rethink our goals and realign our aims... The New Moon is also a time to start new projects, so, during every New Moon (and up to eight hours afterwards) make a list of your Top Ten Wishes for the month. (The New Moons are all listed in the Moon Meditations section from page 77).

Important points about wishing

1. Write down your wishes in a special book—an exercise book will 'do', but why not treat yourself to something a little special? Use coloured pens to make your list look super-special and add doodles and drawings to the words, if you feel inspired.

(Yes, you *can* use a scrap of paper and a plain ol' biro if you're in a hurry, but the more energy you put into your list, the better.) The main thing is to clarify your wishes once a month.

2. When you're making your New Moon wish list, avoid asking for the not-very-likely. For example, instead of 'I wish to be instantly RICH!' try the slightly more realistic 'I wish to save more and spend less' or 'I wish to find a better paid job'.

3. Allow the Universe leeway to deliver the goods. For example, if it's sex and romance you're after, don't put down the name of a specific person you fancy. Instead try something like, 'I wish to find love as soon as it is right for me' or 'I wish to meet someone who loves me as I love them'. Then go deeper. If it's love you're after and you know it's a lack of confidence that's holding you back, use the power of the New Moon to wish for confidence.

4. Now look for ways to make your wishes come true. For example, if you want romance, make sure you get out and shake your booty! If you want a better paid job, tell your friends and start scouring the employment columns.

5. Each month, check your last list to see how many of your wishes have come true, or what you can do about the ones that didn't. Note which ones you can now leave behind, and remember, what will be will be.

DATES OF THE ZODIAC FOR 2004

Aries	21 March—19 April
Taurus	20 April—20 May
Gemini	21 May—21 June
Cancer	22 June—22 July
Leo	23 July—22 August
Virgo	23 August—22 September
Libra	23 September—23 October
Scorpio	24 October—21 November
Sagittarius	22 November—21 December
Capricorn	22 December—19 January
Aquarius	20 January—18 February
Pisces	19 February—20 March

The dates of the zodiac signs vary a little from year to year for reasons too complex to explain here. But if you're born on the 'cusp' (ie: the change-over day), you're not a bit of each Sun sign, you're either one or the other...depending on the exact time, date and place you were born.

If you were born on the 'cusp' and would like confirmation of your sign, email me your time, date and place of birth via my website www.yasminboland.com.

THE LEO CHARACTER

Oh, to be a warm-hearted Leo, admired far and wide, and worthy of our admiration! Leo's ruled by the Sun, arguably the king and key of the zodiac. Unlike the other planets, who sometimes appear to go retrograde (i.e. backwards), that ol' Sun just keeps ticking forwards, day after day. And Leos are like that too. With no time for the past, they are confident and even headstrong, happy to just keep moving forwards, not holding grudges and not looking backwards. Yes, Leos are the pussycats of the zodiac, for sure, but they're also the lions and lionesses. They can chew you up or smother you in warm loving licks that bowl you over. Anybody who's ever loved a Leo knows that to love you is to be in awe of you.

So how do you do the things you do? With a constant vibrancy and passion enough to start a fire. Actors and actresses come under the sign of Leo and it's indeed true that your sign is connected to dramatics. You also like to be centre stage, whether that's on a real stage or just with your pals. And why not? You always have something interesting to say and people's attention is naturally drawn to you. And you love it. Leo is also the sign of the celebrity. So even if you're not famous yet, use your innate Leo talents to shine like a star wherever you go and whatever you do.

But you never just take, take, take. In fact, you are perhaps the most generous sign of the zodiac, giving your time, money and love to anyone you know who needs it. But you're not cheap! Leos treat themselves as well as treating others and you want the best of everything—dinners and cars and bits and bobs—all fit for a king, of course!

When the going gets tough you have another celestial advantage—you can hold your head high and command respect in almost any situation. Sometimes haughty, always dignified, there's rarely any danger of you losing your cool. Although you can be fiery, you don't often let your temper get the better of you (except when confronted by true simpletons, of course!). You like others to know their place and anyone who spends enough time around you, certainly learns it. You know that you're just a little bit different and you like it just like that. Never ordinary, always distinctive, Leo leads.

CAREER 2004

In theory, as the Sun rules Leo, you might stereotypically be expected to be a king, a superstar or an entrepreneur. In practice, you're probably just very lovely to have around any workplace because you're the 'leader' type who knows how to gather the troops into action; who can liven up the day with your dramatics; and who's warmhearted to a fault.

This year could be big on the work front, though how it turns out is up to you. Each year, there is what's called an eclipse season...which occurs when the Full and New Moons take place close to the Lunar Nodes (which are another astro story altogether). And where eclipses go, change follows. Eclipses are fairly unpredictable and throughout history, were considered portends of doom, which you might already know! However, part of the reason (in fact, probably the main reason for this), is that during a total eclipse, the skies go dark and dogs have a habit of yowling ominously. Little wonder that the average peasant, who had no idea when a total eclipse was scheduled, greatly feared them. However the darkened skies don't need to be feared. The main thing is to work with them as much as you can. Forewarned is forearmed and that is really the whole point of reading your 'stars'? An eclipse can pull the rug out from under your feet but usually there are whispers and hints from the Universe about the need to change the rug you're standing on. Does that make sense? So if you have a hint that the rug you're standing on needs changing, you might step aside so that when it's whipped away, you're not tripped over by it. Eclipses will take place in or across your work zone in May and October, which means getting started on your career as soon as the New Year bell tolls.

The Sun in your daily work and health zone in January means turning your eye to the daily grind is a good idea from here onwards. How confident and/or proud do you feel about your working life on a daily basis? Are there areas you would like to improve? If you are looking for work, you may find that now is the time to really concentrate on how you present yourself to potential employers. You don't want to be too arrogant, nor overly confident. The way to do this is to back down from acting out your ego fantasies and maintain a quiet confidence in yourself—just because you know you can do the job. You have the North Node in your career zone at the start of the year, which is good news. This little heavenly point is like a karmic safety net, meaning you can get away with more than most.

MONEY 2004

Jupiter is a very generous planet and being in your cash zone this year, may lead you to over spending. The key this year is to go against the Leo and Jupiter grain and resist buying every little expensive item that catches your eye.

Would you believe me if I told you that you have the ability to make a lot of money this year? Jupiter, which has a very good name for bringing luck, is in your cash zone. So add Jupiter to cash and you get an equation which looks something like this:

If Jupiter $= 4$ and cash $= \$$, then $4 + \$ = \$\$\$$

So that's the good news. The other news you need to know as you start to rub your hands together is that: (a) this transit has actually been with you since September 2003 and that (b) those $\$\$\$$ could be bills. The thing about Jupiter is that he is a very generous planet, and here in your cash zone, he can make you keen and even overly charitable with yourself and others. Given that you are a very generous sign, this can lead to over spending. The key this year is to make sure that you don't just say 'bugger it' and buy every little expensive item that takes your fancy. Uh uh. Instead, go against the Leo and Jupiter grain and resist the temptation to buy the first lavishly luxurious item that catches your eye. Shop around, compare prices and be prepared to haggle if someone looks like they're prepared to barter with you. That way, you safeguard yourself from the possible influence of Jupiter to get you so optimistic about life and your finances that you end up in a financial muddle. So that's the not so good news. Back to $4 + \$ = \$\$\$$. For some Leos, this year will see a serious up-turn in your finances. If so, enjoy it...but set aside a little for a rainy day. Not that I am forecasting a rainy day, but it never hurts to have a little something set aside.

Jupiter in your money chart is also about values. What do you really value and are you doing it justice? Do you in any way feel as though you are 'selling out' and, if so, what are you going to do about it?

LESSONS 2004

It's your responsibility to be…

Wherever Saturn goes, lessons follow. This year, Saturn is hanging out in your solar 12th house. If hippy stuff puts you off, just stop reading now and turn the page—you don't want to know and that's OK. Just take this message with you for 2004—expand your mind and don't be afraid or threatened by its dark corners. If you're not bothered by hippy stuff read on. Saturn in the 12th house is a heavy duty transit but one to relish and make the most of because there is such an enormous ability to grow through it. As well as being a cosmic teacher, Saturn's the grim-faced man with a watch who ticks you off for not keeping up, or for being late. So what's so hippy about that? Hold on. The 12th house is where your most sensitive, delicate and private self dwells. So Saturn passing through your solar 12th house this year means that you could be forgiven for living with a slight, perhaps subconscious, sense of doom. Remember, living as though something good might not happen, or even pessimistically, is ultimately a time waster. So one of your main lessons this year is to enjoy the moment for what it is, without worrying about the future. And here comes the dippy bit. One of the ways to make the most of this transit is to realise that we are not really alone, even though it sometimes feels like it. In new age circles it's said that we are all connected to life everywhere, and getting a sense of this is one of your challenges for the year. Make the most of it. The world might be crazy, and our brains might be vast and sometimes even a little freaky, but realising we are all connected will enable you to live with your new acceptance of yourself.

RELATIONSHIPS 2004

When it comes to relationships, you are the king or queen of it, of course. Yes, Leo is the sign to be adored. You are more than capable of doing the adoring but heck, never, ever in a less than regal fashion. Not to say that you are a love snob, but you do like your lovers to treat you with the kind of respect that you know you deserve.

Not for you are romances that go nowhere with nobodies. Being in love with a Leo is like falling for a superstar. You like good restaurants and fancy nights out. Leave the endless DVD-watching session and pizzas to the other signs.

If your lover needs to win you over, if you're bored with him or her slightly, all he/she needs to do is lavish you with compliments. Go on, admit it. You love to be told how gorgeous you are. The worst thing a lover can do is ignore you. The second worst thing your lover can do is to be dull, boring or drab. You're warm-hearted, magnanimous and generous with those you love...so they should fall into line and consider themselves lucky to be around you.

So what's it going to be? A soul love union or total confusion? With Neptune in your love zone now, the choice is yours. But let's go back a bit. At the start of the year, the planet of chaos and sudden reversals, Uranus, moved into Pisces. What this means to you is that this highly unpredictable (though fun) planet has moved out of your love zone. Uranus does tend to bring chaos, which is why life is exciting when he's around. However, he's also a law unto himself, hell bent on freedom and given to sudden changes of heart. If this sounds anything like your relationships over the past five years, you can bet it's because Uranus has been meddling with the planets on your personal and solar chart. So without wanting to sound too negative, the fact that he's moved out of your 7th house as far as your love life is concerned, really is cause to breathe a sigh of relief. Life may be a little bit more predictable on the love front, but to Leos' ears, that won't sound like a bad thing. Steady and stable doesn't need to mean boring, as you will learn this year.

Having said all that, as one astrological door closes, another one opens, and this year, dreamy Neptune moves into your solar love zone. That's where the soul mate love union comes into the picture. At its highest, Neptune is about spiritual connection, poetry and soul unions. At its worst, it is about confusion and deception. Before you start to worry though, deception includes self-deception, so make self-awareness one of your keywords in romance this year. Romance can make you feel you've inhaled some of the Universe's wacky vibes, but there's always a morning after. This year, aim for a soul union. The New Moon in your solar love zone in February could help kick-start a romance in 2004.

COMPATIBILITY with Other Signs

If you've fallen in love and want to check out your compatibility, read on. But remember, there's more to astrology match-making than just your Sun sign...

LEO–ARIES

In theory, you love each other into a fireball. In practice, you can explode. Sometimes Leo and Aries love each other quickly, sweetly and sharply. While this love affair burns, it burns hot. You adore that Aries won't sit still, but are not quite sure that Aries is giving you enough attention.

LEO–TAURUS

You can't stand it that Taurus sometimes ignores your loudest roars. Taurus can't quite figure out why you want so much attention from him/her. You want to be pampered but Taurus has better things to do. What's more, Taurus thinks you're bossy. You think Taurus is stubborn. Hmmm.

LEO–GEMINI

Gemini knows how to flatter your ego, and that can keep this love alive. But you think Gemini needs more dignity. Can all that ratter-tatter talking be healthy? Gemini loves mind games and can be a little stand-offish. This annoys you because you prefer to be worshipped without question. And yet it can work.

LEO–CANCER
You make Cancer teary. You don't mean to, but sometimes Cancer is so damned touchy and vulnerable that it's inevitable. You like Cancer's loyalty and vice versa. You sometimes scare your Cancer pal, when you shout. If it happens too often, Cancer scuttles away permanently. Leaving you missing being looked after.

LEO–LEO
Think of two stellar personalities and then think about them co-habiting under one roof. Plenty of room for fireworks—and so it is when two Leos hook up. They both think they are the centre of the Universe. So who's right? On the other hand, they also know how to make each other purr.

LEO–VIRGO
You think Virgo spends too long thinking about the duller things in life. Virgo finds you a tad frivolous. You want to be adored and feted at every turn. Virgo doesn't have time for such shenanigans—there are lists to be made, figures to be added up and ideas to be analysed. And yet this one can also work.

LEO–LIBRA
These two can decorate each other into a frenzy. They look more beautiful just by standing next to each other. They're like a celebrity couple whose togetherness boosts their popularity. You do sometimes find Libra just a little bit too cold for comfort and your Libran mate isn't exactly sure why.

LEO–SCORPIO
Both of you are stubborn and when you two clash, things only get worse. You think Scorpio should apologise more often. Scorpio thinks you're crazy— that ain't ever gonna happen. You can't understand why Scorpio holds grudges for so long. Scorpio thinks you should act a little more respectfully. A tricky partnership.

LEO–SAGITTARIUS
You love the Sagittarius get-up-and-go and Sagittarius loves you for being so witty, but you do sometimes want to be stroked a little too much for Sag's taste. You often want more consideration than Sag has to give. Sagittarius has plenty of things to think about aside from you—and you aren't keen on that idea!

LEO–CAPRICORN

You live it up while Capricorn sits around and wonders when the excess is going to stop. You think Capricorn should lighten up, already. Both of you being very ambitious, you both also want centre stage with your careers. But this can be a very sexy combination, making the tougher bits easier to accept.

LEO–AQUARIUS

Opposite might attract, but these two find it hard to stick together. You sit on ceremony and want to be acclaimed. Aquarius has so many things to think about, that sometimes, Aquarius just doesn't find the time to do the adoring. Even so, you appreciate Aquarius' non-clingy style of loving.

LEO–PISCES

Your pride can put Pisces off after a while. You do things without realising that you're trampling over Pisces feelings, and then you refuse to say sorry. You find Pisces alluring...but so disorganised! Pisces can't do it any other way. When you fight, Pisces can go from hot lover to cold fish, which infuriates you.

WEEKLY FORECASTS

2004

—◆—

Week beginning:
4 JANUARY

If someone starts to bug you this week, think of yourself as a naughty school girl or boy who has just been scolded by a teacher. Firstly, you need to consider if, in fact, you have been naughty or if this school teacher (or other authority figure in your life) is just being overly strict. If it's a loved one who has a go, maintain your cheeky schoolies demeanour, but do really think about it if this person has something to teach you. There is a chance this week that the lessons you need to learn are being handed to you on a silver platter—but you aren't ready for them. Either the lessons are not being handed to you on a silver platter, but on a grimy old cracked plate, or the person who's handing them over is grim-faced and not exactly inspiring you into a spirit of cooperation. If that's the case, take the plate and wash it up. Don't let people get you down. You have a lot of good to look forward to this year, so if anyone does try to rain on your parade, tell him or her to take their misery elsewhere. Be optimistic.

See page 79 for your Moon Meditation for this Full Moon

Week beginning:
11 JANUARY

Words are the key to breaking through the mud and getting to the good of a situation this week. Under the Quarter Moon, you need to pick and choose your words carefully. You might be mistaken if you think that losing your temper is going to shock someone into submission, because right now, life is a little unpredictable. Playing it cool while those about you get hot under the collar could be the best idea you've had in years. If you see steam rising, or shooting out of someone's ears, do all you can to bring a lightening bolt of 'sudden peace' to the situation. Do not inflame it. If it's your ears that are getting steamy, do all you can to think about the good things, rather than what's niggling you. While some Leos will be coasting along in their closest one-on-one relationships now, others will be finding that ego issues are getting in the way. If that's the case, take a step back. You do need to be confident. You also need to remember that you are quite an awesome figure when you're fighting fit and make allowances for any mere mortals in your midst who aren't quite keeping up to speed.

Week beginning:
18 JANUARY

Now is a good time to start expressing some of the ideas you have been formulating where your one-on-one relationships are concerned. At the end of 2003 and the beginning of 2004, the questions which started to appear in your mind gave you pause for thought. Now is the time to look back and think about what those questions were—what your answers were and what you are going to do about them. If this seems like a massive task, think about the scientists and engineers who first formulated theories, and what it took to put man on the Moon via a space ship. It must have seemed like a huge ask, so to speak, to be so audacious as to think they could pull off such an amazing feat of engineering. But they did. No doubt they encountered a few nay-sayers along the way, who assured them that they were playing with fire. But unless those conspiracy theories are true, they obviously did pull it off and make the technology. You don't have to figure out how to fly to the Moon this week, but you do need to think about how you can better relate to those nearest and dearest to you.

See page 80 for your Moon Meditation for this New Moon

Week beginning:
25 JANUARY

Last week's New Moon was in your opposite sign, which is why your closest one-on-one relationships were in focus. This week is the start of the rest of your year, in as much as every day is the first day of the rest of your life. If there have been recent dramas that have been doing your head in, now is the time to clean the slate. Slates are pretty good like that. You can scribble all over them and end up with one big mess, but they are also easy to clean. This, of course, doesn't mean that you lose all the info that was on there. Much of it is stored in your memory. You have learnt some important lessons lately, particularly some important lessons about yourself. Now the time has come to use those lessons and a great place to start is to see how much of your own beliefs you are pressing on to someone else. Known as 'projection', it's time to take your ego out of the picture and see how you are conducting yourself with those that matter most. You need to be able to stand up for yourself, but you don't need to push for it too hard.

Week beginning:
1 FEBRUARY

This week under the Full Moon in Leo, give yourself some quality 'me' time. This is not to say that you have to be selfish, but for some unknown reason, you're overly concerned about someone else's wellbeing. Think about this—to be a good friend, lover or co-worker, you do have to be happy in yourself. If that's not a good enough reason to look after yourself, no matter how much of your attention someone else wants, I don't know what is. You are full of empathy for others at the moment—one of the reasons for your popularity—but you also need to think of yourself. If you are giving your energies to someone else because you don't trust yourself or your gut instincts, then you need to think again. It is wonderful to know that you have someone else you can depend on and that you have been a good friend to others recently. This week, let them offer you a helping hand if and when you need it. You don't have to demand it, nor get all passionate or dramatic about having a right to it. In fact, you only need to hint at it, or at least hint until they understand that it's your turn for some nurturing.

See page 81 for your Moon Meditation for this Full Moon

Week beginning:
8 FEBRUARY

Venus has now moved into the part of your chart that governs your philosophies, as well as your studious self. For some, love will come with a foreign flavour; for others, going somewhere foreign will be lovely. Wherever you go and whatever you do, this is a good time to be thinking about standards and integrity. High ideals are wonderful things because they give a straightforward and honest person something to aim for. But obviously not everyone has the same standards. It's not that the week's vibes incline you to be judgmental now, but in striving for high ideals, you may need to make some allowances, especially when it comes to dealing with other people. Sometimes we want something to be so perfect that we're tempted to almost think about trashing the whole idea if imperfections start to raise their head. This is a good week not to do that. In fact, right now, you are in a position to help others feel good about themselves, even if they aren't quite hitting the high marks everyone thinks they should aim for. If someone you know is down on themselves this week because they're not living up to their standards, help them see their value. If someone disappoints you by not living up to your high ideals for them, help them see their value.

Week beginning:
15 FEBRUARY

This week could be quite surprising as your Sun makes a powerful aspect to the planet of the unexpected, Uranus, under the New Moon. Think of yourself as a child just starting out in what they call the pre-verbal stage. You can't speak and you probably don't understand much more than the tones of people's voices. You can hear when people are being caring and when they are not. When you are at this basic stage of life, it's easy to be surprised by the unexpected. It's said that early childhood traumas that we can't even begin to grasp at the time they occur, can affect us later. This is a good time for you to use your ability to understand life as an adult in order to stop experiencing trauma. Sometimes you have problems because you have your intuitive head in the clouds. This week, use your head to understand what's going on rather than allowing it to cut a wound you'll have to deal with later. You know how to do it better than anyone else. Being kind and generous with yourself is a very good idea.

See page 82 for your Moon Meditation for this New Moon

Week beginning:
22 FEBRUARY

You're not the most secretive of types but right now, you could find that you reveal something very interesting about yourself, to someone who matters a lot. A lot of the week's heavenly activity is taking place in your solar 8th house, which governs other people's money. You might find that, in fact, what you reveal is about finances or joint finances. However this part of your solar chart also covers the less easy-to-explain House of Taboos. What do you consider taboo? Everyone has something they feel that they need to hide. How would you feel about revealing at least a glimpse of your shadow self to someone now? You're keener than usual to explore the forbidden in your life now, and while no-one would say 'just let it all hang out, baby' it doesn't hurt, I hope, to suggest that you consider which of your secrets would be worthwhile to reveal. If you think someone has misunderstood you recently, because they are missing a crucial piece of information that might surprise them, consider spilling the beans (responsibly). However, if you are being in any way motivated by jealousy, have a word with yourself before having a word with anyone else.

Week beginning:
29 FEBRUARY

This is a great week to start laying the foundations for what you would like to do with your working life, even if other parts of your existence seem to be crying out for attention. Let other parts of your life go with the flow and start to think about what you would do if you could, at work. In the not too distant future, Venus will be entering your work zone. It could be a lucrative time for you soon, if you play your cards right now. It's a wonderful thing to be blindly optimistic, however it's also good to pay some serious attention to reality every now and then. You have the ability to get people to sign on the dotted line, so if you have a project brewing which you are keen to get off the ground, now is a good time to start laying the groundwork. With Jupiter still going backwards in your cash zone, you have a chance now to earn some money you thought had slipped through your fingers. How confident do you feel about your joint financial arrangements right now? That means taxes, mortgages and salaries. If they could use an overhaul, now is the time.

Week beginning:
7 MARCH

Q: How do you turn up the volume on a Full Moon?
A: Put it near the planet Jupiter.

The Full Moon is in Virgo, your neighbouring sign. To put a traditional spin on it, you might find that a cash deal you have been juggling finally comes to a conclusion around about now. A financial matter could also be settled. There is the possibility of a delay in payment somewhere along the line, so set aside a little cash just in case. However, more important is the question of ego, which is firing up the skies right now and has been for some time. The planet with the big ego, Jupiter, who spent 2002 in your sign, is now in the middle of Virgo and going backwards. Now is a time of money, money, money. New age guru, Deepak Chopra, once told me that people who regard money as dirty will succeed in keeping it away from them. People who accept that money can't buy happiness but acknowledge that it's quite nice to have at the ready, are more likely to draw it to them. With Jupiter in your cash zone and the Full Moon there last week, it's a good time to examine your feelings about money. Draw it to you or push it away, as you wish!

See page 83 for your Moon Meditation for this Full Moon

Week beginning:
14 MARCH

When witches and wiccans want to find the perfect night to cast a spell for love, the more astrologically inclined will look for a night when Venus makes a harmonious aspect to Jupiter on Wednesday. Venus is the love principle and Jupiter is the expansion planet so put them together and you (hopefully) get an expansion of love. This is a great aspect for all the signs. If you happen to know anything about your personal birthchart and you know you have planets or angles at 12 degrees, this will be something you will REALLY feel. If you don't know anything about your birthchart, but wish you did, you can cast it for free at www.astro.com...although it might take some explaining! On your solar chart, though, the Jupiter/Venus love up takes place in the parts of your chart governing work and cash. What this means is not that 'the most amazing thing ever' is going to happen but that your work and cash outlook is very good. If you were thinking about asking for a raise, there could be worse times to do it, but do check your boss's mood first.

Week beginning:
21 MARCH

This week, the Lord of the Underworld and the seriously dark and intense planet, Pluto, starts to go backwards in the skies. Well, actually, he doesn't REALLY go backwards, he just looks like he is, from our standpoint here on Earth. This is called a 'retrograde' in astro speak and is considered very important. Pluto is about change and transformation, getting rid of rubbish and about the healing crisis. As Pluto starts his retrograde motion, he will be storing up energy, to be released when he starts to go forward again in August. For Leo, this is happening in the solar pleasure zone. For many people, creative projects that they have been working on will be due for an overhaul now. Many novelists will tell you, 'it's all in the rewriting' and that could hold true for most creative projects. It's the old 10% inspiration, 90% perspiration thing. If you have been working on a special, creative project of your own, see if you can't revamp it very successfully now. If your project is connected to someone overseas, or from overseas, so much the better. Work on what is important to you ethically.

See page 84 for your Moon Meditation for this New Moon

Week beginning:
28 MARCH

You know you are a big person. Not physically, perhaps, but you have a big personality. Well, most Leos do. Leo isn't the sign of the actor for nothing, you know. You guys have the ability to strut and fret across life's stage like there's no need for actor training. You're the entertainers of the zodiac, with the big hearts and flashy smiles and sometimes even lion manes of hair, which you pride yourself on. This week, though, someone might try to wipe that flashy smile off your face, if you're not careful. I don't mean to alarm you, but there is a distinct possibility that someone perhaps wants a bit of what you've got and in trying to get it, bugs you. It may well be a question of boundaries. If someone is trying to impinge on you now, tell them to take a step back. If you are, in fact, the over-the-boundary-stepper, then rein yourself in. Forgetting who is right and who is wrong, contemplate the idea of boundaries. Your symbol is the Sun and the Sun, as we all know, is king, and rules. The Sun knows no boundaries and just shines away, being deflected but never extinguished except by diurnal rhythms. Remember that.

Week beginning:
4 APRIL

This week, in all matters which confuse you (and there might be a few) you have one simple guideline to follow to get the best results. This is it—if in doubt, let your conscience be your guide. A powerful aspect between your glorious ruler, the Sun, and dreamy Neptune around the time of the Full Moon on the fifth will help us all to use our intuition rather than our ego, to be more selfless. If there's a tricky matter that comes up for you now, ask yourself, what would you do if your ego wasn't involved? What does your 'gut' tell you to do? The trick now is to keep your ego well out of the way, and of course, that is always easier said than done. The problem with egos is that they tend to be so darn large and can obscure important parts of a picture. However, with Mercury in your solar 9th house, you do, at least, have the planet of communications on your side, helping you to see the broader expanse. Your dreams could be quite strong now and they may well be telling you some important information. Or...they could be a clear outline of your perfect fantasies. Discern the difference.

See page 85 for your Moon Meditation for this Full Moon

Week beginning:
11 APRIL

The planet of communication, Mercury, is now retrograde. For some astrologers, Mercury retrograde (aka Mercury Rx) is a time when communication can go haywire, travel plans can be disrupted and computers can do things like crash or explode. Yes, this is all possible. But looking at your solar chart, it's more important for you to use the Mercury Rx energy to reopen your mind to an idea you might have closed to it. For many Leos, it's also going to mean that a trip away that you thought might not happen will come to fruition now. Others may find that a project they had lost faith in lives to see another day. If you're feeling quite philosophical right now, go with it. Expanding your horizons is a lifelong adventure and you don't have to leave home to do it. Reading about the world outside your window can be as mind expanding as taking a trip to a foreign country and immersing yourself in their culture. Doing both is best, of course, but if you can't get away now, enjoy the chance to be an armchair traveller. You could transform your life, as your ruler also aspects the most profound of the planets, Pluto.

Week beginning:
18 APRIL

Watch Out! Watch Out! There's an eclipse about. Actually, you have to love eclipses, they are bolts from the blue which change, if not everything, then something...and something major. Something that needs to be changed and probably won't change back again. This eclipse takes place in the sign of Aries, very close to the planet Mercury. For you this is in your solar 9th house. If you have any outstanding legal matters, they are likely to come to a climax and you should soon get results. If it is not a legal and binding matter that is holding your attention, whatever happens now may not be quite as final as it seems. Because Mercury is still retrograde, this often signifies that matters which are decided now will be reconsidered later. Most astro folk choose not to sign contracts while Mercury is going backwards because they often have to be re-signed later, as new information comes to light. On the other hand, some people prefer to sign up under Mercury Rx because it gives them space for renegotiations later on. Whichever you choose is up to you. Many Leos will have news from afar which seemingly comes from nowhere.

See page 86 for your Moon Meditation for this New Moon

Week beginning:
25 APRIL

If last week's eclipse has taken its toll at all, this is the week to look to your friends for support as Venus and Mars snuggle up in your friends' zone, promising love, support and fun to take your mind off any recent dramas. You're not a great one for withdrawing, although you don't mind licking the odd wound, so turn to your pals if at any point in the week you find yourself in need of support. Your networks and the groups you belong to can be a source of caring. If you need to sort a few confusing things out with friends, this is a good week to take the first step. Your words could change your world now and what you say could have a regenerative effect...either on you or on someone you care a lot about. You have the chance to really look behind someone's shield, to see the real them and to love them flaws and all, if that's how you feel. But you're not going to get there by having superficial conversations all the time, so don't be afraid to go deeper if the moment and the mood are right.

Week beginning:
2 MAY

Venus is still opposite Pluto this week, so power struggles around love and money are still possible. The good news is that Mercury has now begun to move forwards again. If you have been stalling on finalising something, you now know which way you want to proceed. It's pretty much all systems go. The eclipsed Full Moon in your home zone indicates that for many Leos, there is a tension between work and homelife. Perhaps you have been paying too much attention to your career and not enough to your homelife, as far as some people are concerned. Let them think what they like while you take time out to really think about how you feel about the situation. If you find that your ego is getting in the way of your professional life, this is the time to think about what you are going to do about it. It's also a good time to ask yourself how confident you feel about the way you have been tackling your career now and if you don't work, then your reputation and status—the part of you which is recognised for what you do, rather than who you really are. These are all-important issues. But so is your homelife.

See page 87 for your Moon Meditation for this Full Moon

Week beginning:
9 MAY

Last week, power struggles about love, passion and money rose to the surface, and probably around your homelife. This was created by the opposition of the planet Venus to the powerhouse, Pluto, and the eclipse. This week we're left to pick up the pieces. The thing about eclipses is that, sometimes, if we are hanging onto something we shouldn't, we are made to loosen our grip. Have you felt as though you 'should' let go of something (or someone) you were clinging on to? The aim of being wise is probably learning when it's time to let go... Either side of you now, if you check, has two energies—one of which is quite loving and one of which knows how to spin a yarn. This is a very good time to tell someone how you feel. It's also a great time to go away on a short trip somewhere with someone you love, if that's an option. If you are lucky enough to have ongoing love in your life, this is a good time to contemplate it, just quietly. Why not thank your lucky stars? If you stay true to yourself it can get (even) better from here.

Week beginning:
16 MAY

The New Moon this week falls at 28 Taurus and in your work zone. This means that you have a chance to make a fresh start on an important work matter. If you have been waiting for news about your professional life, it could come, if not this week, then very soon indeed. Think back to November 2002. Was there a work matter that was on your mind? There was an eclipse in this spot back then, so for some, this New Moon will be about going forward from a point which you can trace back in time. Even if that's not the case, though, work matters are likely to be the focus now and what you need to apply to them is a lot of confidence and understanding. You're a leader, but if you need some support and nurturing now, don't be afraid to ask for it. If it's not you but an ally who needs a helping hand, once again, don't be afraid to offer it. Mercury moves into Taurus now, joining your Sun in your work zone, so your name may well be on everyone's lips. As far as is Leo-ly possible, please smile and enjoy the attention.

See page 88 for your Moon Meditation for this New Moon

Week beginning:
23 MAY

Last week Mars started moving up towards Saturn. These two meet about once every two years and when they do, the issue of authority is likely to arise in the lives of many. For you, this meeting is taking place in your solar 12th house, which is the house of secrets. If you are being leaned upon to keep something a secret now, make sure you are not being bullied into it. Sometimes people present convincing cases for why you should keep something to yourself, but you are under no obligation to keep anyone else's secrets if you feel it is compromising you. Are you by any chance living with a vague fear about what might happen if you don't do as you are told? If so, stop it immediately. Fear is a waste of time and the most negative of emotions. Emotions are running high right now but there is no need to cave in under them and crumble. You are imbued with an amazing integrity and right now it's your very reliable code of ethics that will help you make the right decisions. Don't beat yourself up for past mistakes. Enjoy this chance to do it right this time. And don't let anyone harangue you.

Week beginning:
30 MAY

Venus opposite Pluto and parallel Mars during this Full Moon week could bring love or money matters to a head now. If you're bamboozled about the best way forward about love or money, don't lose heart or hope because before too long, not only will you be able to understand what the heck is going on, you're going to be able to express it very well indeed. The main drama now is that you know how strong you are, and you know where you should direct your strength, but there is also a sense that you don't want to throw your weight around, and that you shouldn't be forced to 'prove yourself' time and time again. You have already proven yourself, over and over. However, if one last party trick is what it takes to convince certain people that you have what it takes to do what you want, then go ahead, put on a show to win them over. What's that? It's beneath you to have to win people over? Come on. You're only asked to do it every now and then, after all. Go for it. Amaze your critics.

See page 89 for your Moon Meditation for this Full Moon

Week beginning:
6 JUNE

With Venus now going backwards in your solar house of friends, it's time for you to really look at what your friends bring you and what they 'take' from you. I don't mean be mercenary and weigh up their good and bad points and treat them accordingly, but now is a good time to evaluate your friendships and all your close relationships. If you have suffered a past hurt, now is a wonderful time to release it, but don't expect to be able to do some kind of 'new age-y' magical exercise to release it all. It takes more than sitting on a few crystals (or whatever) to really release a hurt. You also need to identify the problem, admit to the hurt, and let it go. Of course you also need to forgive. Try reciting this before you sleep, if there is someone you are struggling to forgive: 'I forgive everyone and everyone forgives me...' Write it down a few times and see how it feels. Sometimes we hold on to angst long after the 'sorrys' have been said. It's time to let something go, as last week's Moon in your fellow Fire sign of Sagittarius takes effect. Let go of resentment, if you have any directed towards someone, especially if it's someone who once meant a lot to you.

Week beginning:
13 JUNE

This week sees a harmonious aspect from the planet of altered states, Neptune, to the Venus/Mercury/Sun line up in Gemini. This is a great week for all the signs to get in touch with their 'higher self'. That's the part of you that isn't worried about getting a seat on the bus in the morning and can marvel at a sunset over the grimiest skyline. It's the part of you that knows what is right. But don't get carried away into the next dimension. Spiritual practices are well starred right now, so if you know how to meditate or practise yoga, now would be a great week for it. That's the good news but I am also duty bound to tell you that this week is also one where we could simply hear what we want to hear, so wash out your ears on a daily basis and run everything you hear via your 'rubbish radar'. Make sure you're on the level yourself. If you've been thinking up an imaginative or poetic idea lately, give it some more thought as there's a lightness of being on the ethers. With Venus still retrograde, it could be an old artistic idea that comes back to you now.

See page 90 for your Moon Meditation for this New Moon

Week beginning:
20 JUNE

If you really want to use the heavenly vibes on offer this week, all you have to do is sign up for your local yoga class. It's that simple. Your spiritual solar 12th house is being activated now and amongst the pack in there is Mars, who loves a bit of sport. Put that together with a bit of spiritual sport, such as yoga, and you could really take a load off your head and feet. In fact, you can think mind, body and spirit now, as the mind planet, Mercury, is also in that secret, sensitive part of you which benefits from such esoteric pursuits as meditation. By Wednesday, Mars will be in your own sign, giving you an energy boost like you haven't had for years. For some Leos, this will make them feel a little edgy, which is all the more reason to make like a pretzel and do yoga (or whatever). For others, it's going to give you the boost you need to take that most important step. If you can have a growing trust in the higher powers at work now, you are using the heavenly vibe.

Week beginning:
27 JUNE

You could really surprise someone this week and, of course, that person could be you. But whomever it is that you decide to turn on the Leo magic for, they are most probably going to enjoy it—perhaps even more so than they first thought they would. How many people you decide to tell about this little incident remains to be seen though, as a matter which causes you to pause for thought this week looks like it could be quite a private issue. It may well be to do with something that you consider intimate or taboo, too. And it may be to do with the issue of freedom. The key this week is to make sure that you don't allow anyone to rain on your parade when it comes to mulling over your most pressing issues. Don't be bullied or bossed around, and think of as many ways as you can to keep things light. Right now you have the ability to see all sides of the story and to look beyond the ironies and the paradoxes to see what really matters. You also have heightened intuition, so if you are in touch with that, use it. You have a chance to express yourself clearly now.

See page 91 for your Moon Meditation for this Full Moon

Week beginning:
4 JULY

Last week's Full Moon may well have brought matters to a head on one important partnership matter. With Venus now direct again and still in your zone of friends, you have a chance to make new friends and appreciate old ones. If you have decided that there are apologies that need to be made, or rifts which you'd like to see healed, now is a good time to make the first move. Your ruler, the Sun, goes over serious Saturn on Thursday—a good time to act like an adult and build bridges. Going slowly but surely might not be what you want to do right now, but if you can manage to slow down a little from that Leo pace of life, you will be surprised at how much there is to see around you. You may feel fenced in, so don't restrict yourself. If you can see that there are bad habits developing in how you spend your time, this is a good week to nip them in the bud. If someone asks you a question that you don't want to answer, ask them, 'Why do you want to know?'

Week beginning:
11 JULY

There's a New Moon at the end of the week as Mercury and Mars snuggle up in your sign. Say what you mean now, but think about what you say. You might as well sort out what needs to be said before the big conversation starts; that way you will be prepared for it and if you're prepared for it, you are far more likely to just sail through it. Not that sailing through something is the only thing to aim for. Obviously, one hopes to learn lessons as one goes on and the New Moon in the most secret part of your chart, near serious Saturn, suggests you have ample opportunity to learn some weighty lessons now. Of course, lessons are only as good as you make them. All the wisdom in the world isn't going to do you any good if you allow it go in one ear and out the other and Mercury and Mars together in your sign, it has to be said, incline you to such folly. Avoid it and instead channel their power more usefully. This is a great week to get a tedious task done, which has been hanging around for too long.

See page 92 for your Moon Meditation for this New Moon

Week beginning:
18 JULY

OK, everyone sing along... 'Ahhhh, love to love you, baby...' Your ruler Mars this week makes a harmonious aspect with its partner and love buddy Venus. OK, again...'Ahhhh, love to love you, baby...' However, at the same time, sweet meek and mild Venus makes a tough aspect to Jupiter. 'Ahhhh, love to love you, baby...' There's not only just enough love to go around right now, there's almost too much of the stuff! Lucky you! Of course, not everybody will experience this energy the same way. This week, despite these decidedly romantic and sexy planets, some people will, for example, be breaking up with loved ones. Divorces don't stop because Venus and Mars and Jupiter are making out, more's the pity. So before I gush about how Venus and Mars can never be just friends, bear with me while I pause to console those in tough love situations. The aspects this week suggest that if love is tricky right now, being motivated to do the right thing could help. Jupiter bestows luck—but maybe the luck in your life means you're being shunted out of a bad relationship so you can get yourself into a better one. If your love life is fine, this week could make it finer. And if your love life is non-existent, the sexy and romantic vibe in the air this week could change all that.

Week beginning:
25 JULY

Glory be to the Lion King, the Sun is back in Leo for another year, which means it's not that long until your birthday…many happy returns. This takes the total tally of planets in Leo (at the start of the week, anyway), to three, as Mars and Mercury are also doing their stuff in your first solar house. For many Leos, love matters relating back as far as June 2002 will come up as Venus passes over the spot made sensitive back then and a Full Moon takes place in your solar 7th house. If there are delays regarding partnership matters now, do all you can to be patient. With Mars still in your sign, this may not be the easiest task you've tackled all year but you will benefit from holding those horses a little bit if you can. The energies are quite strong this week and it's fair to say that speaking rashly is a danger, so do guard against shooting from the lips if there are setbacks to put your nose out of joint. You know you deserve all the respect in the world, so exude the kind of confidence which will attract that, for best results.

See page 93 for your Moon Meditation for this Full Moon

Week beginning:
1 AUGUST

You can persuade people to just about anything now, if you have the courage of your convictions. So do you? Are you roaring away like a nice lion should during his or her birthday month? Or are you doing the meek kitty thing and allowing others to roar at you? If you feel as though you need to overhaul your appearance now, in order to make a better impression on those you are dealing with, the decision to get the mane attended to or to spruce up anything at all which broadcasts your image at work, will pay off nicely. You probably feel as though there are quite a few people about who are keen to judge you and you might be right. However, just because they are judging, doesn't mean you are being judged harshly. Be confident in how you come across right now and if you can't be confident do something about it, so that you can be! Your exterior, the package you present to the world, is on show now more than ever, so lick and polish it while the time is ripe. There are also massive changes afoot, so keep an open mind.

Week beginning:
8 AUGUST

If someone disappoints you this week, don't write them off altogether. OK, if they have been very, very bad, then perhaps they don't deserve any more than a not so fond farewell. However, if they have merely failed to live up to the high ideals you have placed on them, and if you feel in your generous heart and your gut that they are sorry, and they want your forgiveness, by all means, give them another chance. As Mercury starts to go backwards, it will slowly become possible to take back any angry words that you've spat out lately. Right now, you are being guided, so look out for the signs about how you should proceed. If you need to turn your thoughts to your finances now, do so. Mars is about to enter your solar cash zone, so getting your finances in order could start to feel like a pressing priority. Take the initiative with your finances. Reconsider, perhaps, where most of your cash has been going. Have you been spending it wisely and well? Now is also a great time for you to think about what you value—above and beyond cash and possessions.

Week beginning:
15 AUGUST

There's a New Moon in Leo this week and that's good news for you. Not only does it augur well if it's your birthday week, but it's a chance for all Leos to make the fresh start they often find they need around this time of year. Most of you should be recharged and refreshed by now, unless other indicators in your personal chart are outweighing the good times in your solar chart. Why not take this annual New Moon in your sign as a fabulous opportunity to make a list of what you would like to achieve between now and your next birthday? Do it thoroughly too. Make a list, and make it attractive, then put it somewhere you'll remember. In new age, writing things down or saying them out loud is said to be even more powerful than merely thinking of them. You are talking to yourself and even though the cleverest psychologists know this affects us, they don't know how much. The other good thing about goal setting now is that you are marking this New Moon in your sign and jumping on the Leo wave, as it were.

See page 94 for your Moon Meditation for this New Moon

Week beginning:
22 AUGUST

Stephen King wrote a wonderful short story about a man who found he could 'delete' people from his life by writing their name on his computer screen and then hitting delete. Well, that was the bare bones of it. It would be wonderful if we could erase our harshest and angriest words as easily. A few weeks ago, the planet of communications, Mercury, had a face-off with the planet of sudden reversals, Uranus. This took place at the start of the month and now as Mercury continues his retrograde through his home sign of Virgo, the fast pace he's travelling means he's about to face up to Uranus all over again. However, this time he is in his retrograde phase and so for some people, who really do honestly want to mend fences, this week offers a window of opportunity. You can't hit delete and erase the worst of what you said, but you can take it back. If the shoe is on the other foot and someone said something to you that you wish they'd retract, give them half a chance this week and they might do it.

Week beginning:
29 AUGUST

Don't be fooled by the news that the Moon is full in watery Pisces. It's a potentially explosive time for us all. Shadowing the Full Moon is the fact that Mars and the Sun have recently opposed unpredictable Uranus. And Pluto, arguably the most powerful and intense planet of them all, prepares to go forward this week as well. So what does this all mean? Firstly, let's talk about the Full Moon. This means that there are some climaxes and conclusions to be expected now. Questions you have had may now be answered. Projects you have poured energy into may culminate as you see whether your work sinks or swims. If it sinks, don't panic. Mercury Rx means you could easily have a second chance later. Also, the Mars/Sun aspects to Uranus means many of us are keen, maybe too keen, to go it alone and do it ourselves. Standing on your own two feet is a good move. However, don't let your need for independence translate as an angry 'leave me alone, I can do it myself!' outburst. Finally, with Pluto about to go direct, perspective will start to shift. If there is an area of your life where you have been feeling stuck, you may now find that this project starts to go forward.

See page 95 for your Moon Meditation for this Full Moon

Week beginning:
5 SEPTEMBER

Mercury, the planet of communication, is now going forward again and he's about to go into your cash zone. If there has been toing and froing where money is concerned, you will be delighted to hear that matters look like being sorted out. Network and make connections, but don't promise too much. With Jupiter also ensconced in there, as well as the Sun and Mars, it's fair to say that money matters are both spotlighted and well starred. If you have been thinking about setting up future cash foundations, put the basics into place now while you have the get up and go to attend to this mundane but important part of life. A harmonious link from serious Saturn to your cash zone suggests that you can build cash structures that will stand you in good stead in the future. Venus also moves into your sign this week and as she does, she should also help your cash situation to go forward. That happens on Monday and also promises to help you start looking better than you have done in some time. If you worked on attending to your appearance as advised a few weeks ago, but still could do with a little final grooming, do it now.

Week beginning:
12 SEPTEMBER

For you, the planets are lined up in the part of your chart that relates to self-esteem, cash and values, as they have been for a few weeks now. Are you getting the message that the Universe is trying to send you about working hard to get these parts of your life into slick working order while you can? Enormous changes are possible now. The part of your chart being activated is where you keep your assets stored. That includes your worldly possessions and your natural assets, too. The New Moon on Tuesday gives you a chance to start over again where these are concerned, as well as highlighting this part of your life for the next four weeks. If your spending has been getting out of hand, thanks to a dash of Leo extravagance, rein it in, rather than hoping for a miracle. It's not that a miracle won't come, it's that this is a heavenly good time to work through your real life cash dilemmas; and if a cash miracle also happens to pass you by, well, so much the better.

See page 96 for your Moon Meditation for this New Moon

Week beginning:
19 SEPTEMBER

If life seems just too straightforward and boring for words lately, you're going to be happy to hear this. This week, confusion abounds! It's also a potentially antsy week, with the Quarter Moon on the 21st. If you get into a befuddled, confused state this week, try the following—ask yourself what 'love' would do, in the same situation you find yourself in. That, of course, includes self-love. If you really, really loved yourself, what would you do? Love is transformative now, so you can transform yourself with it. Loving yourself is easier this week, for everyone. If someone loves themselves so much that they're getting on your wick, get in touch with that self-love. It's a cliché to say that you can't love anyone else until you love yourself, but it's also true. The Sun, Mars and Jupiter all start to move into Libra now, and as they do, relationship issues are going to be more visible to everyone, as Libra is the sign of partnerships. It's a great time to think about your own relationships and they don't have to be romantic. Make harmony and balance your goals now. Harmony and balance really are out there, just waiting to be plucked from the ethers.

Week beginning:
26 SEPTEMBER

The Full Moon this week will bring one important matter to a climax. If you have a legal matter pending or are waiting on news from overseas, you may get your answers now. This is actually a pretty powerful Full Moon so if you are the type to mark its passing, get your candles out now. A Full Moon often brings matters to a head but it's also the peak of the lunar cycle for another month, so it's a great time to start getting rid of what you no longer need in your life. If you feel more emotional this week, try not to blame others as the Full Moon is likely to stir people up and that includes you, as it opposes your Sun. It's in the sign of Aries which is a fellow Fire sign, so once again, temperatures could rise. However, if you rise too, as in rise above, and allow for the power of the Moon to subside, there should be no harm done. Venus still in your sign is bestowing you with her charms, so make the most of them and flaunt what you've got (in the nicest possible way, of course!). The issue of finances is still in the air and this week provides you with another chance to secure your future, at least to some extent.

See page 97 for your Moon Meditation for this Full Moon

Week beginning:
3 OCTOBER

OK, that's it! It's over for another 18 months. Sorry to say, but Venus has left your sign and moved into Virgo. Oh well. Never mind. How much more indulgence could you have taken, anyway? And of course, as Venus departs, flirtatiously blowing a kiss over her shoulder at you, she leaves you with the blessings she bestowed on you during her time in your sign. These include: vats of newfound charm, truckloads of grace and, hopefully, a new haircut and maybe even a better wardrobe. This is the week, then, to stop preening and start thinking. Turn your mind to your most urgent matter, as the time for really nutting out a problem arrives. Communication with others now rises to the surface for many Leos so if there is an important conversation that you know you need to have, schedule it for this week (it feels right!). Tuesday is an optimum date for that. Some Leos will be planning a short trip and if that's the case, rest assured it is well starred. Just avoid going over the top where love is concerned, especially around Wednesday. There is an eclipse soon, so be forearmed and make your communication crystal clear this week.

Week beginning:
10 OCTOBER

This is an eclipse week and these are weeks that often provide turning points. The eclipse is on the New Moon—when the Sun and Moon pass over the same longitudinal spot in the skies—in the partnership oriented sign of Libra. If you have personal planets in Libra near the 21 degrees mark (find out via www.astro.com), this will be a very important time for you. Even if you don't, you will feel the eclipse because they are powerful celestial moments, and often described as astrological wild cards. On your solar chart, the eclipse falls in your communications zone. This means that what you say now becomes very important, especially as you already have a line-up of heavenly bodies sauntering through this chatty part of your chart. Harsh words with someone a lot older or younger than you are not recommended. If you can hold your tongue until the fever of the eclipse has peaked after Thursday, so much the better. If your tongue does get away with you—or someone else's gets away with them and heads in your direction— see if ego or pride is involved. If you remove ego from the situation, what are you left with?

See page 98 for your Moon Meditation for this New Moon

Week beginning:
17 OCTOBER

If last week's eclipse has left you slightly wobbly, this is the week to be sure that your legs will straighten up soon enough. If something you said has rebounded on you, it isn't necessarily a bad thing. Last week's eclipse did activate your communication zone, and this week the planet of communication, Mercury, meets up with unpredictable Uranus. This could be what the Chinese mean when they say 'may you live in interesting times'. All kinds of communication, from conversations to emails to text messages and beyond could be confusing and/or erratic. It could well be that any harsh words this week will come from someone at home and will be about finances that you share, such as the rent or the mortgage or even just housekeeping money. Try to remember that the mood is high right now, so avoid being swept into anything underhand or which doesn't feel right as the post eclipse Moon makes her way through secretive Scorpio. If there is an important matter you've been keeping a lid on lately, the time to reveal all could be fast approaching. The conversations you have now are very unlikely to be too superficial for your tastes. Think a little deeper than you did before, if you're searching for an answer now. Be discreet.

Week beginning:
24 OCTOBER

One partnership matter looks set to get sorted out now. Not suddenly, you understand, but slowly and surely. Where there has been confusion regarding a past or present lover, you stand a very good chance of finding clarity this week. Though you might not quite get the full story just yet, you look very likely to stumble across a way of understanding your present love dilemma a little bit better. It may be that your partner has been a little evasive and hard to pin down lately. It may be that he or she has needed time alone to contemplate life and the Universe. If this is the case, you may well get him or her 'back' this week as they return from their contemplations. For some Leos, an interesting secret will be revealed. It could be a secret that inspires you, or it could be a little disappointing. The best way to handle it, if and when it comes, is to stay calm and as Zen as you can. Mars in your communication zone is encouraging you to get worked up and certainly some Leos have had reason to do this recently, but if you can avoid anger and work towards good communications, you will be using the heavenly vibe.

See page 99 for your Moon Meditation for this Full Moon

Week beginning:
31 OCTOBER

How good do you want love to be? This week is a potential doozey for many of the signs. There is love aplenty as Venus meets Jupiter. Venus, as you know, is about love, and Jupiter is about expansion so put them together and you get an expanded love, if you're lucky, of course! The only possible problem is that Jupiter can and, often does, overdo things. So don't let too much love spoil your week. Live and let love. Tell those you love that you're brimming with affection. And, of course, remember that self-love is the most important love of all. OK, now that's been said, I'll have to put in a caveat. For one thing, the Venus/Jupiter rendezvous might not translate as love action. It's hard to find a bad side to this transit but Venus is also about money, so in fact, it could be that you get some cash now, or, sorry to say, that some new bills will come in. If you need more time to pay them, you might be in luck, as the week looks good for talking about money in an optimistic frame of mind and frankly, when it comes to talking about money, that's often the best way to do it.

Week beginning:
7 NOVEMBER

There's a New Moon this week in Scorpio, in your 4th house of...yes, you guessed it...home and hearth. For someone who likes to go out and socialise quite often, you're paying a lot of attention to your domestic situation now, and that is potentially a very good thing. Why not have a mini clear out? Go through your junk. You might be amazed at how much freer you feel after this. You could easily find something, as you go through your stuff, to stop and make you smile. With Venus in your communication zone and making a harmonious aspect to Mercury in your creativity zone, now is a great time to kick-start any creative or artistic projects you've had in mind for a while, but haven't got around to doing. Go on, jump on the lunar vibe while you can! The Venus/Mercury meeting also indicates that it's a good time to whisper sweet nothings in the ear of someone who has taken (or takes) your fancy. A little bit of romantic mind play could be quite enjoyable for you now.

See page 100 for your Moon Meditation for this New Moon

Week beginning:
14 NOVEMBER

Time to start rebuilding whatever parts of your life are due for some maintenance. But here's the funny thing about rebuilding—you have to smash down something before you can rebuild it. And, of course, you also have to clear away the debris, before you can start rebuilding. In fact, there are plenty of things that have to happen before you can rebuild anything. Something has to be either broken, demolished or just in need of renovation, before you can rebuild it. It may be that you need to work on letting go of fears, as Saturn goes backwards in the part of your solar chart which deals with the most sensitive part of you. You actually have good stars for working with spiritual energies now, so why not use them? If you decide to do something to your home—or if you are already in the process of doing it—then you could make the cleaning up a bit of an exercise in making a fresh start. Yes, it's nearly the end of the year, and what better time to 'weed the garden' and to get the place in order for next year, than now? And enjoy the Zen moments in between.

Week beginning:
21 NOVEMBER

Try to keep things as sweet as you can this week, as a tough aspect between Venus and Saturn passes by. For some people, there will be a feeling of 'not enough love' in the air. That's like having not enough oxygen, and definitely not something anyone wants for themselves. Feeling like you can't get enough of what you want is annoying, but try to relax a little, like a person in an air pocket who knows that breathing in slowly will conserve the energy until help arrives, as indeed it will. You can really use your brain to get to the bottom of one very important issue now. Thinking deeply will come naturally this week. If you need to use your imagination, you have it on tap. Not in an 'airy fairy', wafty way either, but in an unreal and otherworldly way. Imagine your best possible scenario and then consider what steps you need to take in order to get there. Some Leos will discover a few interesting secrets this week. Make sure you use that information wisely and for the best of all concerned. The Full Moon could help bring one important project to completion now.

See page 101 for your Moon Meditation for this Full Moon

28 NOVEMBER

Some serious tensions are in the skies, which means there will be a lot happening for everyone this week. Trying to get co-operation from others could be like the old proverbial blood and stone exercise. Relief is at hand, but not until next week. Getting drunk, or angry for that matter, will be exhausting and hardly restorative. The Full Moon in Gemini falls in a spot made sensitive for many back in June 2002. For some, any matters that arose then will conclude now. Fruits can be harvested and what hasn't blossomed can be binned. Use the power of the skies this week to move on from whatever you need to. If you manage it, ask yourself where you need to go next. Meanwhile Venus is headed towards her old friend Mars, and for some, that will be as romantic as it sounds. The Male and the Female Principle—that's yin and yang, man and woman—on top of each other could also be quite fiery. Once again, don't let the energies swamp you—go with them. Don't argue for the sake of it. A square to Neptune from Mars means it's going to be a week where people get heated up about the fine line between fact and fiction.

Week beginning:
5 DECEMBER

Venus gets together with Mars in the sexy sign of Scorpio this week. These two planets can never be just friends and in passionate Scorpio, they don't even have a fighting chance. This is a signal for a little of what you fancy. If you're super astro curious, go to www.astro.com and cast your birthchart for free. Now see if any of your planets fall at 15 degrees of anything, but especially of Scorpio, Virgo, Leo, Cancer, Taurus, Pisces, Aquarius or Capricorn. If they do, you're in double delightful trouble and I wish you lots of fun. Last month's eclipse will still be heating up the air. For you, though, retreat should come at home. Yes, Mars in your home zone is stirring things up, but Venus there too means you have a helping hand when it comes to sorting things out. Do whatever you can now to beautify your home environment, so that you have harmonious surroundings. If your surroundings are harmonious, you are going to be far more likely to handle any stress that comes along. A harmonious home won't erase stress, but it will make it easier to deal with, so give your home a little love now.

Week beginning:
12 DECEMBER

Time to start making those New Year's resolutions. If you can't think of one, take a hint from the New Moon this week which falls in the part of your solar chart dealing with the complex combination of kids, creativity and romance. So, firstly, you may find that all your attention is being taken up with kids, either your own or someone else's. It's a good time to act like a kid, as a New Moon works magic here—which is where creativity and romance comes in. Creativity doesn't have to mean standing at an easel while you paint, but it might do. You can be creative in whichever way comes naturally to you. Even if life isn't simple and straight-forward, you can still look for ways to have fun this week. There's almost always one solid opportunity for a laugh. If romance is the order of the day, enjoy! Hopefully your confidence has had a recent boost, but if it hasn't, then think about how you can make it happen. Take a risk! There are some things that are going to take time, so you might as well allow them to mature and ripen in their own time and enjoy the moment(s) as and when you can.

See page 102 for your Moon Meditation for this New Moon

Week beginning:
19 DECEMBER

A line-up of planets in Sagittarius is creating a party mood, while a tense Saturn/Chiron opposition means there are still some people, of all signs, dealing with some serious old wounds. This is the best time for that kind of thing because just around the corner is the New Year and you can resolve not to do the things which lead to hurt again. One way to withstand the slings and arrows is to be of a strong mind and healthy body. With the Sun about to make her annual appearance in the well-being section of your solar chart, you now have the celestial assistance you need to put new health practices into place. What you really need to do, though, is to work out that gritty little private issue which has been waking you up at night, or at least giving you pause for thought during the day. Once you have that sorted out in your own mind, and once you have decided on the best course of action, you can get back to appreciating those around you and enjoying the end of the year in Leo style—with a big smile and lots of friends around you. If you're sexy but single and looking for love, this could be a good week.

Week beginning:
26 DECEMBER

No-one understands the expression, 'if you've got it, flaunt it' better than a Leo at his or her best. If that's you, start flaunting it, baby, because the planets are on your side and even your harshest critics will have to admit that you are looking good now. In a physical sense, you are exuding a happy air. Well, let's hope so. If life has been tough of late, do all you can to get in touch with Venus and Mars, who are currently hoping for a party in your solar pleasure zone, waiting for you to go out and flirt and have as much fun as possible. If you have had a sniff of romance and you're hoping something more may develop, this could be your lucky week. Strut your stuff. If you've got romance already, this is the week to enjoy it. Go for a mini break somewhere, if you can, or at least spend time enjoying your partner and getting to know them more, as the case may be. This is a time to be optimistic. You have celestial permission to put any major projects on hold while large parts of the world go on holidays, if only for a few days. Enjoy!

See page 103 for your Moon Meditation for this Full Moon

MOON MEDITATIONS
2004

<hr />

MOON MEDITATIONS BY THE MONTH

As the Moon goes around the zodiac each month, she picks up the vibes of the planets she passes and triggers the effects they are having on each other. The state of the skies at the time of the New Moon and Full Moon are especially important, and marks a monthly astrological turning point. These Moon Meditations are written to give you a flavour of the vibe of each New Moon and Full Moon, and to give advice on the right moves to make under each 'lunation'.

NOTE: The time of the Full or New Moon changes depending on where you are in the world. For this reason I haven't given specific times, but simply the relevant dates on which the Full or New Moon may fall depending on your location. For instance, the January Full Moon occurs on 7 January (e.g. Australia, New Zealand) or 8 January (e.g. United Kingdom, United States of America). Visit my website at www.yasminboland.com for accurate information about Moon timings.

7 or 8* January
Full Moon in Cancer

Moon Meditation: 'I ask only that which I need to know…'

Sometimes we want nothing more than to get to the heart of the matter. We go digging for information. Some people call it snooping. But did you ever hear of anyone who went snooping and found something they were glad to get hold of? It's rare (though it does happen…sometimes.) But right now, if you find out all the facts, do you think that will finally make you happy? Far better to focus your energies just before and after this lunation on the healing vibes in the air. Concentrate less on what you think you need to find out and more on how to heal what you already know. Let it go and see what happens next.

A good time to: Spend time with your family,
heal your hurts at home with people you love

* Please see note on page 78

21 or 22* January
New Moon in Aquarius

Moon Meditation: 'Sens-suuu-ality is mine...'

Taking control of a situation sometimes feels like an all-important objective—like the person who thinks that their lover might leave them, and so rushes out the door first, just for the pleasure of knowing that *they* did the dumping. But it's not always the best way of handling things. *Talking* tricky matters through seriously would be a better solution. Any New Moon is a chance to refocus. This New Moon is in exciting Aquarius. It's time to get in touch with what's unique about you; to think originally; and to see if you can't work out a new solution to an old problem which leaves everyone feeling better. Ask around for advice.

A good time to: Love like you've never loved before

* Please see note on page 78

6 February
Full Moon in Leo

Moon Meditation: 'One bright idea can save the day...'

It's only February but already a lot seems to have changed. What appeared so clear is now in doubt. The questions to ask yourself now include: Are my ideals too high? Have I been realistic in my recent aims? This Full Moon is potentially quite a confusing and volatile one. The good news is that one brilliant idea around this Full Moon could sort out a lot. Put your thinking cap on for a few days to change something that needs to. If you wake up at night with a stunning answer to what's perplexing you, write it down. If someone says something that makes a whole lot of sense, heed their words and act on them as soon as possible.

A good time to: Be brash and bold and to show the world how warm-hearted and smart you can be

20 February
New Moon in Pisces

Moon Meditation: 'Come out and dream with me...'

If you're a dreamer, this is your lucky week. This New Moon takes place as the planet of love, Venus, makes a harmonious aspect to the dreamiest planet of them all, Neptune. If you have dreams, allow them to float into the ethers now, where they may be turned magically into a reality. If it's romance you have in mind, scheduling that all-important rendezvous on or just after this date is ideal. Some people will feel as though they have found their soul mates now...and they may be right. Allow yourself to be touched in the softest and most vulnerable way. This is a week to make your dreams real and to change everything by letting someone know you love them.

A good time to: Fantasise, write poetry, drink fine wine, fall in love, get married and live happily

6 or 7* March
Full Moon in Virgo

Moon Meditation: 'I know what I want and what I want is...'

If you have a bone you want to pick with someone, this is a good week for it. Once you've raked over the details and sorted out the loose ends, though, it's time to let it go. This Full Moon is about finishing off outstanding matters and then letting them lie. But before you do that, use the Lunar vibe to get into a spirited and enjoyable discussion about what you know has to be understood more clearly. Use the current clear thinking vibe to unravel a puzzle and your quick wit to get your life in order, with a little help from your friends. Avoid being unnecessarily critical of others right now. But do fight for the truth.

A good time to: Analyse something which has been perplexing you. Check the details

* Please see note on page 78

20 or 21* March
New Moon in Aries

Moon Meditation: 'This is what I'm really like…nowadays…'

Sometimes, meek and mild people go off and do those 'assertiveness training' courses. They return to normal life with a new determination to get what they want. Having spent their life hanging back in the shadows, they suddenly find their tongue and start demanding this, that and all the rights, right now and thank yous. This lunation offers us all a sort of free assertiveness training moment. It's time to stand up for yourself and to go for what you want. But you don't have to demand. Ask gently and see how easily it comes to you now. 0 Aries is the first degree of the zodiac. If you need a fresh slate, you have it. Enjoy it!

A good time to: Get fired up about something you're passionate about. Go for it. Start anew

* Please see note on page 78

5 April
Full Moon in Libra

Moon Meditation: 'I fight only for what's right…'

Mars, the planet with more va-va-voom than a Ferrari showroom, makes a tough angle to Jupiter, the planet that expands everything it touches, so there could be a little bit of feistiness in the air this week—or a lot! For some people, a need to conquer others will arise now, which is not a great situation to have the world in! Are you one of those people racing through life trying to defeat your enemies? The Moon in gentle and partnership-oriented Libra suggests that finding balance now is far more important than getting one over someone else. Don't leave things to chance and don't demand more than your partner, friends or colleagues are prepared to give. Fight for justice.

A good time to: Let go of old arguments and enjoy
a peaceful life with someone you love

19 April
New Moon in Aries

Moon Meditation: 'Because I love you…'

This eclipse week, prepare yourself for the unexpected. In fact, why not take the initiative and surprise yourself. If you know that you could be nicer, sweeter and generally all-round more pleasant to the people you share your life with, this is the week to make that happen. Write a list of 8 people you love, and then think of at least one gorgeous thing you can do for each of them. Now add at least two more people to that list with whom you haven't been getting along with too well lately. Surprise them with a random act of kindness, too. Love can dissolve all barriers now. Go easy as the energies are high. Don't expect anything in return…yet.

A good time to: Get motivated, to be artistic,
to go to an art gallery and to be brave

4 or 5* May
Full Moon in Scorpio

Moon Meditation: 'No more wishful thinking, baby cakes...'

Eclipses are about beginnings and endings. They are astrological wild cards and it's hard to predict which way they're going to go. If you are curious about astrology, go to www.astro.com now and cast your chart for free. Now see if you have any planets between 9 and 19 degrees of Scorpio, Taurus, Aquarius or Leo. If you do, this could be a wiiiiild time for you. If you don't, it still could be that you are dealing with someone whose chart is being super-charged by this eclipsed Full Moon. The way to ride the energies is to let go of what you know is nothing more than a fantasy. If you know it's just wishful thinking, send it on its way.

A good time to: Tell the truth, get to the bottom of something and get very, very sexy

* Please see note on page 78

19 May
New Moon in Taurus

*Moon Meditation: 'Let me take you somewhere
a little off the beaten track...'*

The flavour of this Moon is slow and steady, but a stunning link between Mars and Uranus begs to differ and says we should all trust our decision-making powers now. If you're struck by a brilliant idea, don't discount it just because it came to you in a flash. It *could* be the best idea you've had all year. Once you've decided that it's worth running with, stick to it. This is also a very sensual and even sexual New Moon, so if your love life has been a little dull lately, look to the power of the Heavens and think about new ways to spice it up. Somewhere outdoors with your lover could be more exciting than you expect!

*A good time to: Trust your intuition, roll around
in the grass with someone you fancy*

3 June
Full Moon in Sagittarius

Moon Meditation: 'Sometimes I love completely...or not at all'

On the surface, life might seem just fine—or even better than that. The Moon in Sagittarius has a habit of lightening the times, making the day go faster and parties more fun. But under this Full Moon are undercurrents that we all need to be aware of. The planet of love, Venus, is opposing the passionate and powerful Pluto. This is a day when fun and superficialities won't satisfy our deeper needs. Venus is retrograde right now, so it's a perfect time to re-evaluate your relationships and to look at what they're costing you, versus what they're giving you. Be brave enough to look at this carefully.

A good time to: Throw a Devils and Angels party, allow love to transform you and go deeper

17 or 18* June
New Moon in Gemini

Moon Meditation: 'My message to you is...'

The Sun, Moon and Mercury are now all together in the sign of Gemini. This puts the accent firmly on communications and thought. Since the Sun is about the 'self' this is a good time to ask yourself what you think about yourself—but don't be a harsh critic. This is a New Moon and it's about moving forward. Think about what you like about yourself, rather than anything else. If there are people around you who just don't seem to understand you now, try to help them out. It's possible to make changes now, even if they feel awkward. Start by altering your perception of yourself, then see what you can do to alter others' incorrect perceptions of you.

A good time to: Talk, talk, talk and do some deep thinking.
Then talk some more

* Please see note on page 78

2 July
Full Moon in Capricorn

Moon Meditation: 'Gotta start somewhere…'

The Moon is full in the serious sign of Capricorn, which is governed by Saturn, the teacher of the zodiac. He wants us to deal with hard facts and rewards us for hard work and for those times when we face up to what's required of us. Set against this are two lovely celestial configurations which make it much easier than usual to get things done—as long as we actually get up and do them. And that's the trick right now. In order to get something done, we have to start somewhere. The struggle between homelife and career is also highlighted under this lunation. Is there an area in your life where you need to find some balance? This Full Moon gives you that opportunity.

*A good time to: Build now for a better future
and to mix reality with intuition*

17 July
New Moon in Cancer

Moon Meditation: 'Mmmm, you look good to me...'

If it's love you're longing for, look no further than this New Moon. There are loads of very romantic aspects about, including one between Venus and Mars, the zodiac's lovers. If you've been lusting after someone, this could be the week when you get to satisfy that craving. Of course, there's more to romantic love than just the lusty bits, which is where the aspect between sweet Venus and dreamy Neptune comes into the picture. This aspect is about as romantic as it gets and encourages us all to dream of love. But it doesn't stop there. A third important aspect between Mars and Neptune means we're all being given the celestial opportunity to go chasing our dreams. Enjoy.

*A good time to: Make your move, wear something
a little revealing and merge with someone*

31 July or 1* August
Full Moon in Aquarius

Moon Meditation: 'Did I say that...?'

Be careful which battles you choose this week. One word out of place could bounce back at you quicker than you can say, 'as ye sow, so shall ye reap'. As the Full Moon dawns, talkative Mercury makes a tough angle to the planet of shocks and surprises, Uranus. With emotions running high anyway, there is every chance that people are going to tire of being patient and just blurt out what's on their mind. Just when you least expect it, someone could come up to you and tell you exactly what's on their mind. Or you might do the same to someone else. Make sure it's not just Full Moon madness that is making you prone to blurting. Sudden insights abound.

A good time to: Wake up, wake someone else up,
think clearly and be mentally flexible

* Please see note on page 78

16 August
New Moon in Leo

Moon Meditation: 'Don't get mad nor even…'

The atmosphere around this lunation is quite feisty, quite alive and in many ways spoiling for a fight. Is that you? What a shame to waste the power of a New Moon on negative emotions. Instead of looking for someone to argue with now, we'd all do much better to do something active. The planet that rules sport, Mars, is now at odds with unpredictable Uranus, which means that there's a fight or flight atmosphere. Flight is the best option. Make love not war. It's important to avoid being rebellious for the sake of it right now, despite temptations. Exercise a little caution and remember that Mercury retrograde is probably more to blame for any minor confusion than you are.

A good time to: Take up boxercise and attend to your physical needs as much as your emotional ones

30 August
Full Moon in Pisces

Moon Meditation: 'Emotional fireworks can be very noisy…'

If you're longing for freedom now, use the tensions of this dynamic Full Moon to grab it and run with it. But, before you head out that door, check you've thought it through. The Moon and Uranus now combine to incline us all to a little more than usual 'emotional fireworks'. Are you sure you'll feel the same way next week as you do now? If you can't put your hand on your heart and say 'yes' to that, perhaps it's the Full Moon that's getting you churned up. If this is the case, you'd be well advised to count to a very high number before you act. Avoid doing anything rash, despite the Lunar vibe, which is encouraging all kinds of outbursts.

A good time to: To keep your cool if someone's acting a little emotionally unpredictable

14 or 15* September
New Moon in Virgo

Moon Meditation: 'It's all in the details...'

Serious Saturn gets a bad rap in some astro circles, but he's one of the good guys, really. He just wants the world to face the harsh realities rather than living in fantasy. If you're prone to drifting off into La La Land, use this energised New Moon to commit to reality, at least for the next four weeks. The Moon is in Virgo— a wonderfully down-to-earth, no frills sign—and at the time of the lunation, Saturn is throwing his weight around, sending out a call for all to work hard now for results later. Pour the Lunar energy into something sturdy and constructive, which you know you'll be able to count on in the future.

A good time to: Make a list of your aims,
analyse your ambitions and chase your goals

* Please see note on page 78

28 September
Full Moon in Aries

Moon Meditation: 'Ch-ch-ch-ch-changes...'

Change can be awkward but that doesn't mean we should back off from it. Right now plentiful Jupiter is making a tricky angle to the planet Uranus, who doesn't like anything to stay the same. For many, there are forced changes in the air—some of us have backed ourselves into a corner and are now looking for a window to escape through. But there's no easy way out. It's time to make the tweaks you know you need. Don't worry, changing something doesn't mean leaving it behind completely. And once the changes are in place, life is going to feel one heck of a lot more comfortable. If you have to let something go now, let it go gently.

A good time to: Let off some steam and wonder how you can make the world you want for yourself

14 October
New Moon in Libra

Moon Meditation: 'Never mind the past,
here come the eclipses...'

As the planets move around the skies, they 'touch' each other, making easy and tough angles with one another. It's not that often that they are not 'touching' at least one other planet, and yet under this eclipsed New Moon, both sweet Venus and happy Jupiter are free-standing. This purifies the Venus and Jupiter concepts. This week could see many changes—eclipses almost always do—and yet there is more than just a little light at the end of the tunnel—there's a positive glare! If tensions get too high, try to avoid lecturing someone. Yes, he or she probably does need a piece of your mind, but this may not be the week to give it to them. Be nice to your partner.

A good time to: Truly love someone. Allow changes
within your relationship. Speak softly

28 October
Full Moon in Taurus

Moon Meditation: 'Truly loving can be
a sobering experience...'

Have you been good or bad recently? Go on, be honest. If Santa was to come down your chimney during this eclipsed Full Moon, would you get a sack full of presents or a bag full of coal? This New Moon has karmic overtones and for many of us, it's time for our karmic rewards...or lack thereof! Be honest with yourself about how you've been behaving recently and make up for your 'sins' if need be. Love thyself, but make it tough love. A link between Venus and Saturn now says caring, faithfulness and commitment can save the day. But if those qualities are lacking in a love or friendship-based relationship, it might be time to let it go. Avoid possessiveness.

A good time to: Show someone how loyal you can be
and then to let them decide what to do next...

12 or 13* November
New Moon in Scorpio

Moon Meditation: 'Careful, someone might hear you...'

If you want something, you can go behind the scenes and get sneaky to make it happen, and with the New Moon in Scorpio now, you may well be tempted to take that route. However, it's certainly not the easiest way to go about achieving that ambition which is so close to your heart. After all, if you're too darn secretive about what you want, you run the risk of leaving others in the dark. And if others don't know what you want, how can they possibly help you out? Far better now to be up-front and to use the power of the Mars/Lunar Node to be assertive and to go after what you want in a way that leaves no one guessing.

A good time to: Get Scorpionically sexy, renew your sex life and chase a dream with renewed vigour

* Please see note on page 78

26 or 27* November
Full Moon in Gemini

Moon Meditation: 'I live and I let live...'

It's all very well being idealistic, but don't let your expectations lead you towards disappointment now. That sounds as though this Full Moon is fraught with potential disillusionment but it's not at all. It is highly charged with the possibility that we get so caught up in dreams of our own making that we fail to notice what's going on under our own nose and which needs our attention. This is a very spiritual lunation, make no mistake. And if you need help from someone now, you are likely to get it. Just don't expect too much from yourself or others. Live and let live. Don't idealise others now either. Yes they're wonderful. But no one is perfect. Allow them a little leeway.

A good time to: Say what you need to say and then let others speak their piece. Cruise

* Please see note on page 78

12 December
New Moon in Sagittarius

Moon Meditation: 'True love doesn't have to be crazy love…'

Hold on to your hats because this New Moon occurs in the same place in the skies as powerful Pluto, which means intense times are ahead. Bad intense? Not at all. But it is time to have a look at the emotional investments you've been making and to see what is or isn't working for you. It's once again time for tough love. If someone isn't being a good friend, for example, it's time to let them know where you stand. If your partner's been acting up, be honest about what you need and lay down new ground rules. Venus and Saturn are combining to create firm new ground for us all to walk on where love is concerned.

A good time to: Take love more seriously, to experience love profoundly and to ditch wasted love

26 or 27* December
Full Moon in Cancer

Moon Meditation: 'Have I told you lately…?'

Turn your thoughts to the nest now, and see what feathering you need to do there. It could be that your family, your flatmate, your partner, or even just your furry friend needs some attention now. Under this last Full Moon of the year, Mercury and Venus are meeting up, making it a whole lot easier for us all to communicate our love for those around us, and heck, Christmas has to be a good time for that. If this time of the year is tough on you, the good news is that (a) it won't last forever and (b) if you reach out to someone now and let them know you need some loving, they are astro likely to oblige.

A good time to: Tell someone you love them, spread Christmas cheer and call someone who means the world to you

* Please see note on page 78

About Yasmin Boland

Yasmin Boland started writing as a pre-teen and hasn't stopped. She became a journalist at 20 and quickly decamped to London, where she freelanced for magazines and newspapers including *Elle*, *She*, *B*, *Just 17*, *The Daily Mirror*, *The Evening Standard*, *Playboy*, *New Woman* and *Vogue*. Her love of 'the Stars' began after she returned to Australia in the 90s. Today, she writes weekly columns for magazines and newspapers in the UK and Australia. Yasmin is also the author of *Cosmic Love*, a new guide to attracting love into your life, using the 'ologies' (astrology, numerology, crystalogy and more). Her first novel *Carole King Is An Alien* was released in Australia and the UK in 2000 and her second novel *All The Rage* in 2003. You can visit her website on www.yasminboland.com.